DESTINATION MARS

LIVING ON
MARS

Ty Chapman

Lerner Publications ◆ Minneapolis

Lerner Publications Company
An imprint of Lerner Publishing Group, Inc.
241 First Avenue North
Minneapolis, MN 55401 USA

For reading levels and more information, look up this title at www.lernerbooks.com.

Main body text set in Aptifer Sans LT Pro.
Typeface provided by Linotype AG.

Designer: Viet Chu **Photo Editor:** Annie Zheng

Library of Congress Cataloging-in-Publication Data

Names: Chapman, Ty, author.
Title: Living on Mars / Ty Chapman.
Description: Minneapolis, MN, USA : Lerner Publications Company, an imprint
   of Lerner Publishing Group, Inc., [2024] | Series: Destination Mars. Alternator
   books | Includes bibliographical references and index. | Audience: Ages 8–12 |
   Audience: Grades 4–6 | Summary: "Explore the obstacles humans would face if
   they were to try living on Mars. Those who've wondered how we'd eat or breathe
   on the red planet will want to dig in!"— Provided by publisher.
Identifiers: LCCN 2022043354 (print) | LCCN 2022043355
   (ebook) | ISBN 9781728490656 (lib. bdg.) | ISBN 9798765602782 (pbk.) |
   ISBN 9781728496900 (EB PDF)
Subjects: LCSH: Mars (Planet) | Space colonies. | Planets—Environmental
   engineering.
Classification: LCC TL795.7 .C43 2024 (print) | LCC TL795.7 (ebook) |
   DDC 629.45/53—dc23/eng/20221020

LC record available at https://lccn.loc.gov/2022043354
LC ebook record available at https://lccn.loc.gov/2022043355

Manufactured in the United States of America
2-1010773-51014-3/12/2024

TABLE OF CONTENTS

Buzz Aldrin sets up equipment on the moon's surface and measures its underground activity.

INTRODUCTION
LIFE AMONG THE STARS

Living on Mars might seem like science fiction, but before the 1960s, so did landing on the moon. On July 20, 1969, two astronauts from the United States National Aeronautics and Space Administration (NASA), Neil Armstrong and Edwin "Buzz" Aldrin, became the first humans to walk on the moon's surface. They planted a US flag in the lifeless regolith (a material that covers rock on the moon) as proof of their journey. It was a massive success for NASA. Since then, ten more humans have traveled to the moon in many space missions.

The first moon landing proved that humans could travel to other planets. Many people began wondering where we would go next. Scientists at NASA quickly began working on space missions to Mars. They developed rovers to study our neighboring planet. They need to understand everything they can about Mars before they send humans to live there. The more scientists learn, the more challenges they encounter and have to overcome.

With recent advancements in technology and new scientific discoveries, colonies of astronauts living and working on Mars might one day become a reality. Can human beings truly live on Mars?

Scientists do not yet know what the bases on Mars will look like.

NASA used space shuttles to send astronauts and supplies into space from 1981 to 2011.

CHAPTER 1

GETTING TO MARS

Before scientists can put entire colonies on Mars, they need to figure out how to build a single base on the planet's surface. Of course, long before they can create anything on Mars, they need to figure out how to get to the planet more quickly.

A one-way trip to Mars, according to NASA, takes about seven months. These trips send rovers and other spacecraft to the planet for exploration and study. But unpiloted spacecraft do not need to return to Earth. They explore Mars until their instruments stop working. A round trip, where humans go to Mars and later return to Earth, would likely take at least three years. This includes traveling time, as well as time spent learning and studying on the planet.

Astronauts wear protective gear and safety straps when they launch into space. The spacecraft shakes, makes loud noises, and puts a lot of pressure on their bodies as it travels through the atmosphere.

Three years might not sound like a long time for space travel, but all people, even astronauts, have basic human needs. A spacecraft journeying to Mars needs to bring enough food and water for the astronauts to survive their trip. A group of four astronauts on a three-year mission to the Red Planet would require about 3,000 gallons (11,356 l) of water and 24,000 pounds (10,886 kg) of food. Some spacecraft can

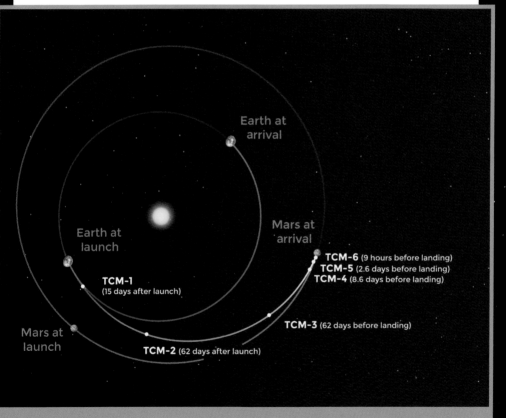

Earth at arrival

Earth at launch

Mars at arrival

TCM-6 (9 hours before landing)
TCM-5 (2.6 days before landing)
TCM-4 (8.6 days before landing)

TCM-1
(15 days after launch)

TCM-3 (62 days before landing)

Mars at launch

TCM-2 (62 days after launch)

This diagram shows the path (*white*) that a spacecraft takes as it travels from Earth to Mars.

In November 2022, NASA successfully launched its newest rocket, Artemis 1. Artemis is the most powerful rocket in the world.

The Orion spacecraft can carry up to six astronauts at once. The first Orion mission including astronauts is scheduled for May 2024.

carry even more astronauts, so they would have to carry more food and water too. These heavy supplies would take up a large amount of room on any spacecraft and require a lot of power to launch into space.

HELP IS FAR AWAY

Apollo 13 was a NASA mission to land astronauts on the moon. Partway to the moon, one of the spacecraft's oxygen tanks suddenly exploded. Ground controllers sprang into action to help the Apollo crew. Thanks to their swift response, the astronauts made it home safely.

If an emergency happens on a mission to Mars, the trip home would take longer. The astronauts might run out of food and water. NASA is working hard to prepare for emergencies.

On April 17, 1970, three astronauts on Apollo 13 landed safely in the Pacific Ocean and were rescued by US Navy officers.

FUELING UP

A spacecraft on a round trip to Mars would need to bring enough fuel for the entire journey. Shipping 1 ton (0.9 t) of resources to Mars requires roughly 225 tons (204 t) of fuel. This is inefficient and very expensive. One solution is to have the astronauts make more fuel once they arrive on the planet. That way they only need to bring enough to get to Mars.

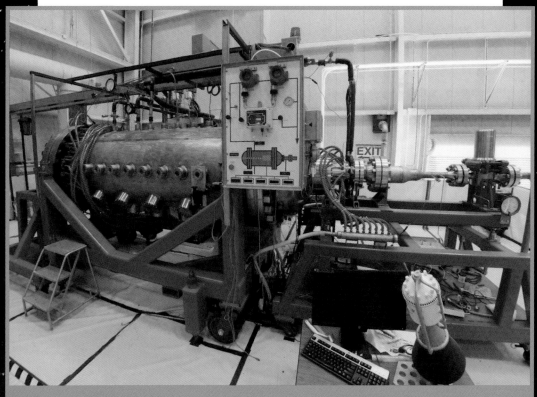

NASA tests new kinds of rockets and fuels in their laboratories. They want to make a rocket that is powerful enough to send humans to Mars.

Future spacecraft may be powered by splitting atoms, very small particles of material. Splitting atoms creates a lot of energy.

Scientists are still uncertain how astronauts on Mars could make spacecraft fuel. The European Space Agency is working on a system powered by sunlight that creates fuel from water and carbon dioxide.

Some engineers have a different idea. They believe they can send certain microbes to Mars instead of fuel. When the microbes consume carbon dioxide, they create new chemicals that astronauts on Mars can turn into fuel.

SAFE DESCENT

Space agencies have successfully landed rovers on Mars's surface many times. However, the spacecraft used to transport human beings to Mars would be much larger than the craft used to land rovers. These larger spacecraft require new, stronger equipment and technology to make sure astronauts land safely.

Scientists at NASA have already begun developing new safety equipment. A landing spacecraft can get as hot as 2,370°F (1,299°C). When rovers land, they are protected by a heat shield. But a rover's heat shield is too small to protect a

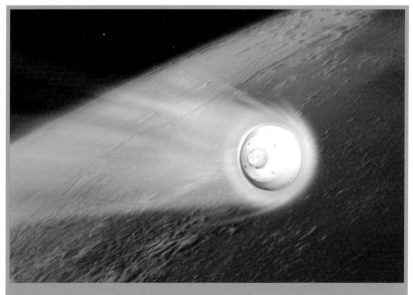

When the spacecraft carrying the rover Perseverance arrived at Mars, it was traveling nearly 12,500 miles (20,116 km) per hour. The heat shield helps slow the spacecraft so that it lands gently on the surface.

Perseverance's heat shield was about 15 feet (4.6 m) across.

spacecraft carrying humans. NASA is working on creating an inflatable heat shield that will protect a crew as they descend through Mars's atmosphere. They have also developed new space suits that work in harsh places, such as the surface of Mars. The new space suits are more flexible and have better communication systems than the old suits.

While NASA is developing technology and equipment to make crewed missions to Mars possible, it'll be a while before scientists have everything figured out. And getting there is only step one.

Astronauts on Mars can help repair rovers and travel to places that robots cannot reach.

CHAPTER 2
THE GRAND CHALLENGE

If landing on Mars is a challenge, *living* on the planet is a truly grand one. First, scientists have not yet created rockets that are strong enough to send one spacecraft containing the astronauts and all the supplies they need for their mission. Anyone who tries living on the planet's surface might have to depend on shipments of supplies being delivered from Earth.

But spacecraft can take over half a year to travel the 140 million miles (225 million km) from Earth to Mars. Many things could go wrong with the shipments along the way. If anything did go wrong, help would also take a long time to arrive.

To provide food for humans on Mars, scientists are thinking

Astronauts will need to travel in groups so that they can help one another in emergencies.

Due to the frequent dust storms that block sunlight, a greenhouse may not work on Mars. It may have to be in orbit instead.

about using greenhouses. Astronauts could build greenhouses on Mars to grow their own food. Seeds require less fuel to send to Mars than fruits and vegetables do.

But how would astronauts grow food? Mars's soil contains chlorine, a chemical that can be toxic to living things. Because of the high amounts of chlorine in Mars's soil, growing food will be very difficult. To solve this problem, a group of researchers used materials on Earth to create soil that is just like the soil found on Mars. They tested and discovered a way to remove chlorine and other harmful chemicals from the soil.

The Biosphere 2 laboratory ran an experiment to see if humans could grow enough food without any outside help. The experiment was successful. It showed that humans could survive in a base on a lifeless planet by growing their own crops.

With the right equipment, astronauts on Mars might be able to use Martian soil to grow food.

Martian soil is reddish in color because it contains a lot of iron rust.

LIVING IN SPACE IS HARD

The International Space Station (ISS) is the largest space station orbiting Earth. It provides a laboratory for astronauts to conduct research in space. The ISS has taught scientists how living in space affects the human body and mind. Scientists better understand space radiation due to research from the ISS. Life in space can be very lonely, so astronauts bring entertainment with them. With no gravity on board, astronauts must exercise regularly to avoid losing too much weight.

Although living on the ISS is challenging, astronauts also get the unique experience of seeing Earth from space.

SURVIVING ON THE RED PLANET

Bad soil and distance aren't the only problems astronauts would face living on the planet's surface. Mars's atmosphere is mostly carbon dioxide, a gas humans cannot breathe. They need to bring oxygen with them. They may also be able to create oxygen once they are on Mars. The Perseverance rover carries a tool called MOXIE that can convert Martian air into breathable air. Humans on Mars might use a bigger version of MOXIE.

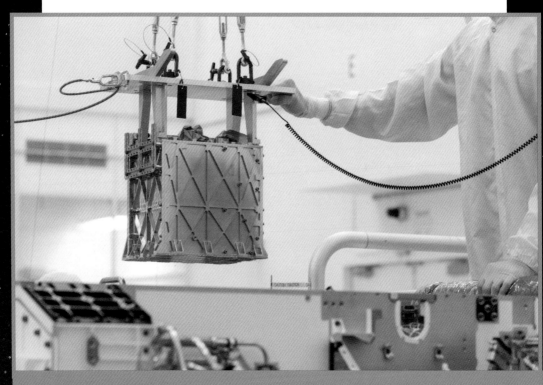

Perseverance's MOXIE tool is a golden box about the size of a microwave. It is a powerful piece of equipment even though it is so small.

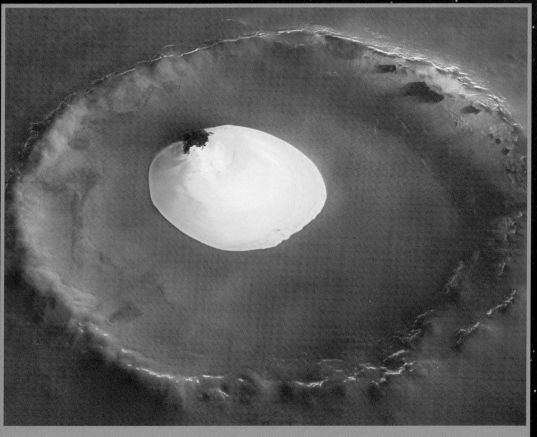

Some places on Mars have patches of frozen water, such as in this crater.

Mars also has no potable (safe to drink) liquid water. Most of the water on Mars is frozen. It lies under the soil and in the ice at Mars's north and south poles. Astronauts need to bring liquid water with them to survive. But they might be able to dig up frozen water on Mars. Recent data from an orbiter showed scientists that there may be liquid lakes under the ice at Mars's poles.

Curiosity measures radiation on Mars, giving scientists important
data that they can use to help plan human missions.

The surface of Mars is constantly exposed to radiation from the sun and other stars. The total amount of radiation spells disaster for any human being's health. Space travelers on Mars need special protective gear. Their laboratories, greenhouses, and shelters need thick walls made of protective material.

PARTS OF A SPACE SUIT

A spacesuit can have up to **16 LAYERS**

Cooling Garment

Underneath the thick outer layer of the space suit, astronauts wear a thinner cooling layer that protects them from overheating.

Communication

Space suits contain radios so astronauts can communicate with others on the spacecraft or with mission controllers on Earth.

Gloves

Thick gloves keep astronauts' hands warm.

Display Control Module

Astronauts can control the life-support system using the panel on their chest.

Colored Stripes

Each astronaut has unique colored stripes so others can identify them.

Helmet

A helmet protects astronauts from the sun's rays.

Portable Life Support System

The backpack on a space suit contains the astronaut's life-support system.

Hard Upper Torso

The hard upper torso connects the space suit to the life-support system.

Lower Torso

The lower torso is where astronauts carry their tools and attach the tether that keeps them connected to the spacecraft.

Scientists test space suits and other equipment here on Earth. They work in rocky, dry places that are similar to Mars. They practice taking data and driving rovers.

CHAPTER 3
SOLVING PROBLEMS

Scientists across the globe are working tirelessly to solve the problems humans on Mars will face. NASA is developing stronger rockets to speed up the travel time to Mars and back. A faster journey means the astronauts don't need as much food, water, and other supplies. It will also help keep the astronauts from getting bored or lonely.

Mars's surface is covered in rusty red dust. When strong winds blow, the dust swirls into the air and blocks sunlight. So astronauts living on Mars cannot rely on solar power. A power outage due to a dust storm can be dangerous. NASA is testing other sources of energy to reduce the chance of power outages on Mars.

A Martian dust storm can reach several miles into the air. The Opportunity rover shut down for good when a dust storm blocked the sun.

NASA is also testing lasers to communicate with astronauts instead of radios. Lasers can contain more data than radio signals can. Astronauts on Mars will send a laser signal to a spacecraft that orbits Mars. Then the orbiter will send the signal to a receiver on Earth. This important technology will help scientists on Earth talk with astronauts and assist them with any problems or emergencies they might face. Astronauts

NASA plans on setting up laser communications throughout the solar system so that astronauts on future missions can send large amounts of data back to Earth.

Charles Bolden (*left*), then NASA administrator, has a video call with two astronauts aboard the ISS. NASA published a recording of the call so people could see how scientists on Earth communicate with astronauts.

will be able to make calls home to family members and check in with doctors. They will also send scientific data to Earth.

Visits to Mars are still a long way out. Going to the Red Planet won't be as easy as sending humans to the moon. Scientists are hard at work trying to solve problems and develop new technology. While there is still much to figure out, humanity has never been closer to living among the stars.

Glossary

atmosphere: the layer of gases that surrounds a planet

carbon dioxide: a gas formed when humans breathe out, which plants use to make oxygen

chlorine: a chemical that can be harmful to living things and is commonly used in bleach or to disinfect water

colony: a group of people who settle together in a new place

consume: to take in, to eat

ground controller: someone who works in the Mission Control Center to guide spacecraft

orbiter: a spacecraft that travels in space around a planet

oxygen: a chemical found in Earth's atmosphere that humans need to breathe

potable: safe to drink

radiation: strong energy that comes from the sun and other stars

regolith: loose rock, mineral, and glass fragments that cover solid rock on the moon or a planet

Learn More

All about Mars
https://spaceplace.nasa.gov/all-about-mars/en/

Bolte, Mari. *Earth vs. Mars*. Ann Arbor, MI: Cherry Lake, 2022.

Colonization of Mars Facts for Kids
https://kids.kiddle.co/Colonization_of_Mars

Hirsch, Rebecca E. *Mysteries of Mars*. Minneapolis: Lerner Publications, 2021.

Life on Mars
https://www.timeforkids.com/g56/life-on-mars-2/?rl=en-910

Mann, Dionna L. *Hidden Heroes in Space Exploration*. Minneapolis: Lerner Publications, 2023.

Mars—NASA Solar System Exploration
https://solarsystem.nasa.gov/planets/mars/overview/

Ventura, Marne. *The Planets*. Lake Elmo, MN: Focus Readers, 2023.

Index

Photo Acknowledgments

Image credits: NASA, pp. 4, 11, 13, 21, 25, 26; Stephane Masclaux/Shutterstock, p. 5; NASA/Bill Ingalls, p. 6; Official SpaceX Photos/flickr (CC BY-NC 2.0), p. 7; NASA/JPL-Caltech, p. 8; NASA/Joel Kowsky, p. 9; NASA/Robert Markowitz, p. 10; NASA/Mick Speer, p. 12; NASA/JPL-Caltech, p. 14; NASA/JPL-Caltech/Lockheed Martin, p. 15; e71lena/iStock/Getty Images, p. 16; Gorodenkoff/Shutterstock, p. 17; onurdongel/iStock/Getty Images, p. 18; DrStarbuck/Wikimedia Commons (CC BY 2.0), p. 19; Mark Garlick/Science Photo Library/Getty Images, p. 20; NASA/JPL-Caltech, p. 22; ESA/DLR/Freie Universitat Berlin (G. Neukum) (CC BY 4.0), p. 23; NASA/JPL-Caltech/MSSS, p. 24; Aurelian Popescu/500px Unreleased/Getty Images, p. 27; NASA/JPL-Caltech, p. 28; NASA/MSFC/Emmett Given, p. 29. Design elements: SA/DLR/FU-Berlin (CC BY 4.0).

Front cover: Dotted Yeti/Shutterstock.

Back cover: SA/DLR/FU-Berlin (CC BY 4.0).